Flea Market Finds

WITH MATTHEW MEAD

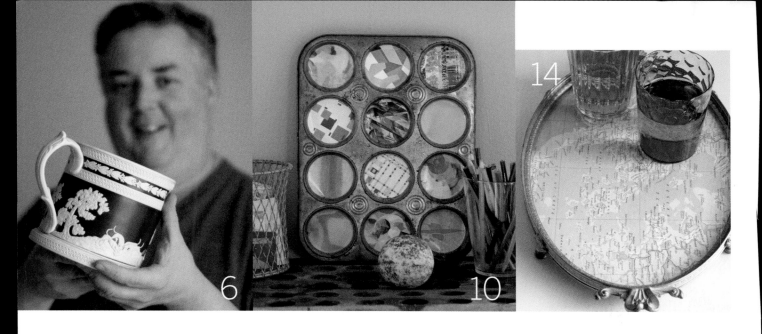

Flea Market Finds
WITH MATTHEW MEAD

ALL PHOTOGRAPHY BY MATTHEW MEAD UNLESS OTHERWISE NOTED.

TIME HOME ENTERTAINMENT

Publisher Richard Fraiman

Vice President, Business Development & Strategy Steven Sandonato

Executive Director, Marketing Services Carol Pittard

Executive Director, Retail & Special Sales Tom Mifsud

Executive Director, New Product Development Peter Harper

Editorial Director Stephen Koepp

Director, Bookazine Development & Marketing Laura Adam

Publishing Director Joy Butts

Finance Director Glenn Buonocore

Assistant General Counsel Helen Wan

Design & Prepress Manager Anne-Michelle Gallero

Brand Manager Nina Fleishman

Associate Production Manager Kimberly Marshall

SPECIAL THANKS TO
Christine Austin, Jeremy Biloon, Jim Childs, Susan Chodakiewicz, Rose Cirrincione, Jacqueline Fitzgerald, Carrie Hertan, Christine Font, Lauren Hall, Suzanne Janso, Mona Li, Robert Marasco, Amy Migliaccio, Nina Mistry, Dave Rozzelle, Ilene Schreider, Adriana Tierno, Alex Voznesenskiy, Vanessa Wu

Flea Market Finds
WITH MATTHEW MEAD

Founder, Creative Director, Editor in Chief Matthew Mead

Managing Editor Jennifer Mead

Executive Editor Linda MacDonald

Senior Writer Sarah Egge

Contributing Lifestyle Editor Stephanie Nielson

Art Director Doug Turshen

Graphic Designer David Huang

Studio Assistants/Designers Lisa Bisson and Lisa Smith-Renauld

SPECIAL THANKS TO
Holly Becker, Jessica Bennett, Kim Demmon, Mary Engelbreit, Tricia Foley, Annette Joseph, Amy Locurto, Sally McElroy, Stephanie Nielson and family, Layla Palmer, Marian Parsons, Kate Riley, Stefanie Schiada, Jocie Sinauer, Mary and Gordon Welch

MODELS
Avery French-Henderson, Sophie MacDonald, Maggie MacLean

With any craft project, check product labels to make sure that the materials you use are safe and nontoxic. The instructions in this book are intended to be followed with adult supervision.

NOTE: Neither the publisher not the author is responsible for your specific health or allergy needs that may require medical supervision, or for any adverse reactions to the recipes contained in this book.

ISBN 10: 1-60320-918-2
ISBN 13: 978-1-60320-918-2

editor's letter

THE FLEA MARKET IS A COMMUNITY of like-minded people. Dealers, shoppers, collectors, the curious, and the clever all come together to sell, accumulate, gather, and exchange. It is also a community of objects and inspiration – a smorgasbord of color, style, pattern, and pedigree. It is where I go to experience things that are current and familiar to me, juxtaposed with items that speak to me from the past. I believe that the flea market represents the original "green" lifestyle — a place where items are re-used, recycled, and refurbished with a nod to their past but with a rich, new purpose. This treasure hunt has become a way of life for me as I collect, prop, and color my life and work with all of the intricate items that can be found there. To purists seeking antiques, the search is for items at least a century old. Vintage aficionados like me are satisfied with objects that are decades old or simply created during our childhoods.

In this issue, we strive to uncover what the perfect "finds" at the flea market might mean for you. Tucked into our pages is an unofficial guide to choosing everything from industrial furnishings and light fixtures to vintage paper and books. We hope you will glean inspiration from our color palettes, fabrics, and the favorite finds of our stylish friends. In essence, we hope you enjoy the thrill of the hunt and our ideas for incorporating your flea market finds into your home.

Keep up with FLEA MARKET FINDS and all of my passions and pursuits at www.HolidayWithMatthewMead.com

And find us on **facebook** at Holiday with Matthew Mead.

FAVORITE FINDS

Unearth the stories behind our beloved flea market treasures.

MATTHEW
What qualifies as flea market bliss in Matthew's life is rooting through a dinged-up carton of "smalls" or pushing past a prominent display to snag a bargain tucked behind. That's what happened recently at The Fairgrounds Antiques market in Swanzey, New Hampshire, when he pulled out this Copeland pottery hunt cup, a trophy-type prize dating back to the heyday of English pottery and the likes of Wedgwood and Spode. It's in perfect condition— and cost just $7. The white designs in relief against a dark chocolate background appeal to his eye. "It has a graphic quality that's very contemporary," he says. "I like all kinds of things, but I love it when I find something that's old but looks modern." PHOTO BY JENNY MEAD

KIM DEMMON

The tale that spins around the table in Kim Demmon's dining room (left) is probably Hollywood fiction, but Kim enjoys telling it. At first, it didn't look like the table was for sale at a small flea market in Camas, Washington, five years ago. "But then the 70-year-old woman started to tell us that the table was once owned by a movie star who had it in her home in the Poconos. And her daughter reminded her it was Katharine Hepburn," says Kim, the stylish blogger behind TodaysCreativeBlog.net. "I quickly bought it. I mostly love her legs." For $200, Kim brought home the table, four chairs, and no extension leaf—but a possible link to Hollywood royalty. PHOTO BY LARA BLAIR

KATE RILEY

Each year on September 5th, Kate Riley and her husband Matt mark their wedding anniversary with a special tradition. "We share a bottle of Champagne and toast all of our successes from the past year," she says. They raise an imperfect pair ("One has a slightly smaller bowl and rim—that's mine," Kate says) of vintage Empoli Italian cased glass goblets (right) that caught Kate's eye 10 years ago in The End of History shop in New York City. It's a go-to source for the kind of vintage glassware and ceramics that Kate entertains with, and the sort of place she features on her popular design-on-a-budget blog, CentsationalGirl.com. PHOTO BY NATE RILEY

MARIAN PARSONS

"I am drawn to antiques that were once utilitarian, but can now be enjoyed for their aesthetic value," says Marian Parsons. As an antiques dealer, author, furniture refurbisher, and blogger (MissMustardSeed.com), she is an all-around expert on vintage and repurposed furnishings. It's not just any old knickknack that's going to get her excited in the way this antique deli scale did. "It looks great in a vignette with other items of age and character," she says. It also does a stand-up job supporting a row of books in her home office. Other functional finds that might someday be Marian's favorites? Fans and typewriters. PHOTO BY KIM WAGNER

TRICIA FOLEY

Tricia Foley can thank the weather for her discovery (left). During the Farmington Antiques Weekend in Connecticut two years ago, it started to rain. "I ducked into a tent to take cover," she says. "Everyone was packing up, but I spied this bowl and had to have it!" The enormous concrete-resin piece was once a garden planter. It was a hefty purchase, but not expensive. "They gave me a discount because it was too heavy to carry back to the parking lot," she says. She drove her car through the mud to get to it, a worthwhile effort for the designer, author, and prolific blogger (TriciaFoley. com) to capture the striking piece that she uses as a serving bowl at parties or simply as sculpture. PHOTO BY AMANDA CAMODEO

AMY LOCURTO

Often, favorite finds have sentimental attachment. Such is the case for graphic designer and blogger Amy Locurto (LivingLocurto.com and PrintablesbyAmy. com). "I always look for cute vintage aprons when I go to flea markets or antiques stores," she says. "They remind me of my little Grandma Chunkie, who had pink-tinted hair and was so fun loving and whimsical. She gave me the love of baking." Amy cherishes the red apron she wore when she helped Grandma Chunkie bake pies (right), and is continually hunting similar retro-looking aprons, dishcloths, and napkins to match. "I love knowing someone's grandma probably made it." PHOTO BY AMY LOCURTO

ANNETTE JOSEPH

Sought-after photo-stylist Annette Joseph (AJPhotostylist.net) has no trouble favoring one of her many vintage treasures above the others. It's this storied country pitcher (left) that dates back to 15th Century France. "The patina is perfect," she says of the ceramic vessel's crackled finish. "It is my favorite shade of green. The pitcher is rustic, colorful, and textural. It defines my style." She'll even reveal that she purchased it at a flea market in Nice, France. But that's all the information you'll get. As a designer who prepares rooms for magazine photo shoots, props sets for TV shows, and even decorates the homes of movie stars, she does not reveal the state-side sources for her fabulous finds. "I have my super-secret vendors—shhh!" she says. PHOTO BY FRANK R. JOSEPH

MARY ENGELBREIT

"If I like something, I don't really care when it was made or where it came from," says artist and magazine editor Mary Engelbreit (MaryEngelbreit.com). So the specific details of her beloved celluloid birdcages (left) are not important to her—nor does it matter that only one plays birdsong when she winds it up. The first one of her pair was a gift from a friend, and Mary sleuthed the second one out in a little antiques shop in Hermann, Missouri. They perch on a table in her home studio, offering cheerful, colorful inspiration. "I'd love to find at least one more," she says wistfully. "If I had three, I'd hang them in my living room window!" PHOTO BY BARBARA MARTIN

HOLLY BECKER

Holly Becker's passion for vintage fabrics and linens gives her passport a workout. A year and a half ago, she traveled to Istanbul and foraged through the markets in the Sultanahmet district to find two unique additions to her collection: the vibrant pieces she holds in her lap (right). "I love vintage ethnic textiles and adore pairing them with new things," she says. "I think that having only new, perfect items in a home is boring. You need patina, worn edges, and a little imperfection to make a home feel authentic." When she was planning a bedroom redo, Holly, the style guru behind the closely followed design blog Decor8blog.com, turned to these textiles for inspiration. PHOTO BY THORSTEN BECKER

STEFANIE SCHIADA

Visitors to Stefanie Schiada's popular blog, Brooklyn Limestone (www.BrooklynLimestone.com) are treated to a pictorial guide through her and husband Luke's renovation saga. Their more-than-100-year-old house started as an ugly duckling, and Stefanie's beautiful photographs chart its progress to gorgeous swan, hinting that camerawork might be one of her additional talents. This vintage camera (left), which she picked up at a burrough flea market, is just for looks. "My favorite find is really my whole camera collection," she says. They are a reminder that technology evolves, but pretty images last forever. PHOTO BY STEFANIE SCHIADA

CLIP ART

You can have an art-filled home without needing the lifestyle or pocketbook of a museum patron. Just turn the pages of secondhand textbooks into creative décor.

COLORFUL COLLAGE

Coffee table books, pamphlets from museum openings, and texts for Art History 101 (opposite) are inexpensive at flea markets, yard sales, and charity book drives. With a pair of scissors or scrapbook punches, you can snip their pages into new masterpieces. To turn a vintage muffin tin into a clever home office or kitchen display (this page), Matthew measured the diameter of the cups, cut circles of modern art prints to fit, and popped them in—no gluing necessary.

NEW SHOWCASES An old glass paperweight gets a makeover (above). If there is any original paper left, remove it and clean the glass. Then cut a favorite print to size and adhere it with découpage medium, such as ModPodge®, or any crafts glue that dries clear. An old drawer serves as a bin for notebooks and journals (below). Freshen the pulls by sticking medallions of art in the centers. Adhere the paper circles using découpage medium, then coat the surface of the paper with more clear-drying medium to protect them and give them a glossy finish.

QUICK FRAME-UPS
Create larger works by grouping several small, page-size reproductions together. Here, four different works are cut and glued into a grid on a rectangle of cardstock. Use a floating frame or document frame to showcase the piece.

WORLD HUES

Chart a course to refreshing style using
vintage globes and maps as inspiration for
cool palettes and projects.

COLORFUL SPINS

Take your favorite vintage globe on a trip to the home center's paint aisle to match colors directly to the hues on the orb. If you can't find ready-made paint chips that coordinate with its aged palette, hand the globe over to the experts to computer-match it. Hues that match this globe are used to give two separate pieces of furniture a unifying new look (this page), turning a two-drawer desk and four-drawer dresser into a tall chest. Cut the legs off the chest of drawers so it rests flat on the desk, and secure the pieces using metal T-brackets screwed to the back. Add loads more storage for pretty Bristol and milk glass pieces with a floating glass shelf that rests on the desk's stretchers. Have the glass cut to fit at a hardware or glass store, and ask for a piece that's at least ½-inch thick. For paint colors (opposite), turn to page 16.

FIT TO PRINT Using five to seven different colors pulled from the globe design, fill the nooks and crannies of a printer's tray to make standout art for the mantel or an entry-table display piece (above, left). Give the old wood a base coat of pale gray or white, and then fill in the colors in a random pattern to get this graphic look.

ALL RISE Once used to elevate food on a buffet table, this wood pedestal (above, right) is the kind of quirky item you'll only find at an antiques store or flea market. Give it some fresh flair with new paint colors (opposite), and employ it on your own table or as a coffee-and-breakfast tray.

GLOBAL PALETTE The various paint colors used on these projects are seen in total on page 14. Clockwise from top, left: Australian Green, Melville, Glorious Sky, Split Pea, Light Sage, Equator Blue, Port Hope, and, in the center, Ocean Blue. The table surface is painted Silver Dollar. For manufacturer names and custom-mix formulations you can take to your favorite paint store, turn to page 158.

"Using a globe for color inspiration leads me to fresh paint hues for transforming furniture. It also helps me be choosy about what I collect. If a piece of pottery doesn't suit the color scheme, I will pass it up." — *Matthew*

AWASH WITH COLOR

Whether you use them to show off a collection of themed pottery or find them appealing on furnishings and room accents, there's plenty to love in water hues.

1. A grommet gives this old wall shelf a stylish new way to hang. Drill a hole ¼-inch smaller than the circumference of the grommet, and then hammer the grommet into place using a rubber mallet. **2.** With an aqua wall as a bold backdrop, the shapely shelf displays rare Akro agate glass flowerpots in gorgeous lake-green hues. **3.** Tall and portable, a metal washstand can serve many purposes.

OPPOSITE: With a coat of fresh color, it performs aptly as a bar. The color wash is a translucent mix of equal parts water and latex paint in soft Mediterranean blue. Depending on the depth of color you want to achieve, you may need to apply several coats. When the stand is dry, stack it with sundries for cocktails, including a bar cloth folded over the towel rack.

BRIGHT IDEA A secondhand atlas (above, left) is fodder for clever paper projects. For this faceted lampshade (above, right), adhere its pages to pressure-sensitive Styrene(R), which is a sticky, plastic-like sheet for sale through crafts stores and lamp-making web sites, such as LampShop.com. Trim the edges with ribbon adhered with crafts glue.

GLASS ACTS Fancy dresser trays or "pin trays" that once adorned vanities and sewing tables can be resurrected as drink trays (opposite). Remove the glass panes and cut an atlas page to the same size and shape. Sandwich it between the panes and place them back in the frame.

TIP: Give a gift that is personally meaningful by trapping a map under glass that shows an ancestral home or the location of a memorable trip.

ABOUT FACE

For some flea market shoppers, haggling is the best part. Even if you're not practiced at negotiating, picking out an item with cracks, stains, or damage is a good place to start talking down the price. **1.** After bringing home this 1960s-era beverage service tray, Matthew and his team addressed its many age-related issues. To make it sturdy, they shored up the top using paint sticks trimmed down to size as structural support beams. **2.** Where the plywood had started to split, they inserted wood glue and held the layers together with bulldog clips until dry. **3.** A coat of Matthew's preferred latex primer, Bulls Eye 1-2-3®, readies the piece for a spiffy new paint job. **OPPOSITE:** With the repairs complete, the beverage tray resumes service, stocked with small glasses and dishes to hold accoutrements.

"Items that show a little wear and tear will be a bargain at flea markets—don't be afraid to pick them up. With patience, some glue, and little repair know-how, you can transform them into something fresh and useful."

— *Matthew*

TO A TEA Who recognizes this ubiquitous dorm-room CD rack (above, left)? Available at nearly any garage sale and thrift store, it rarely costs more than a couple of dollars. With a bit more investment, it can have new life as a spiffy beverage rack for the kitchen counter or a guest room. Start by priming and painting it using a sand-color spray formulated for metals (above, right). While it dries, measure the shelves and ask the local glass store to cut pieces of ocean-blue glass. Finally, stack it with all your tea-making necessities.

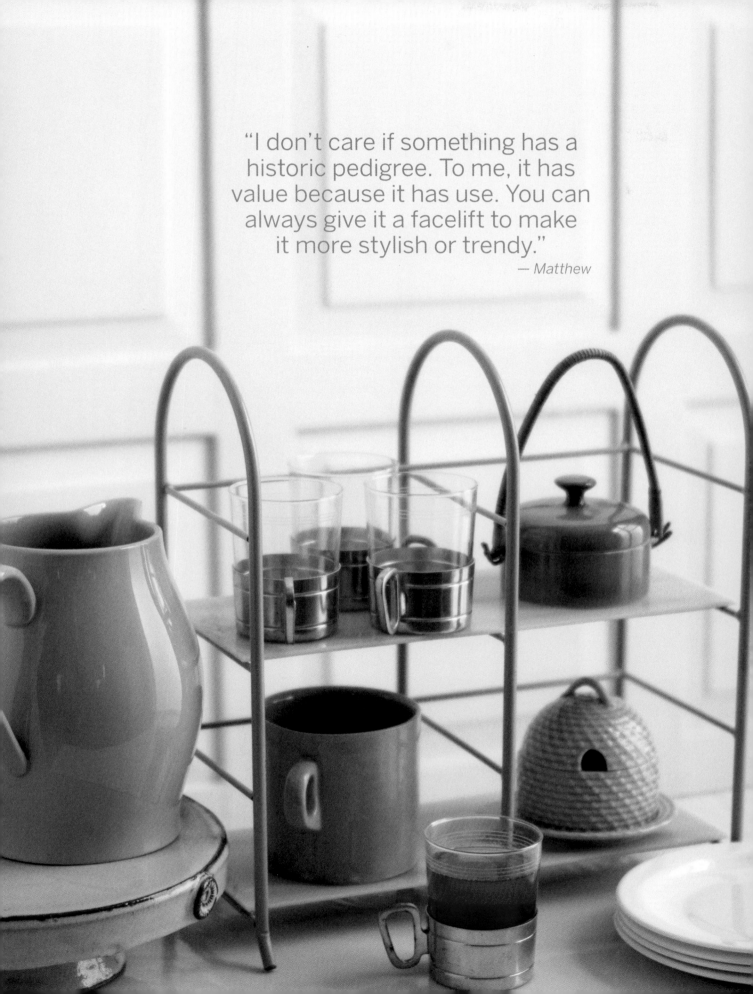

"I don't care if something has a historic pedigree. To me, it has value because it has use. You can always give it a facelift to make it more stylish or trendy."

— *Matthew*

LILAC TIME

It seems that spring-blooming lilacs burst forth suddenly, and then vanish quickly. But you can capture their delicate fragrance and hues, and draw out the season a bit longer with these ideas and collectibles.

CATCH A CHILL

Create a stunning bottle chiller using lilac-filled ice. Form a mold by nestling an empty bottle into a larger metal or plastic cylinder. Fill the gap two-thirds full with water, and insert lilac blossoms. Freeze overnight; then run the mold under lukewarm tap water for 30 seconds, or until you can pull the ice free. Nestle a carafe of water, distilled vodka, or white wine in the chiller, and enjoy.

PIN IT TO YOUR CHEST

Give a plain-Jane bureau a colorful new look. To start, remove knobs (to replace when you're finished), and wipe the piece clean with a damp rag. Choose a lilac-pattern paper, such as wallpaper or wrapping paper, and trim it to fit each drawer or the entire façade. Inspired by the pattern on a vintage plate, Matthew took a close-up photo of the design, enlarged it on the computer, and had a copy center print it on poster-size paper. To adhere the paper, brush on a thick layer of découpage medium (Matthew recommends ModPodge®), smooth out any bubbles, and then apply another coat of medium to seal the top.

MORE THAN JUST PROPS
Vases of lush blooms are favorite subjects for Sunday painters. Their works are plentiful at flea markets, where Matthew looks for canvases and boards that are unframed and therefore inexpensive. Prop the art on a table against a wall, and add lilac-hue collectibles, such as these transferware bowls and a cold-cream jar, to the pretty vignette.

GATHER A BUNCH The state flower of New Hampshire, where Matthew and Jenny grew up and make their home, is the lilac (above). "So the few weeks in May when they are blooming is precious here," he says. To share the bounty from his backyard bushes with the neighbors, Matthew wraps up small bouquets in vintage purple and pink napkins, which he hunts all year long from the odds and ends of mismatched linens at estate sales (opposite). Inside the napkins, water-filled floral picks from the craft store keep the blossoms fresh.

TIP Once cut, lilacs will bloom longer if you smash the woody stems with a hammer so they absorb more water.

I HAVE A PASSION FOR PURPLE

The first lilac bush I ever bought was at a flea market. Most people assume flea markets are only filled with secondhand cast-offs and occasional treasures fished out only by professional dealers, but the truth is that there are also all kinds of seasonal plants and garden materials mixed in—and anyone can bring them home. At the flea market in Davisville, New Hampshire, I go back to one particular vendor every spring because he sells the antique varieties of lilacs that he digs from his own yard. You just won't find bushes like these at the garden center. Happy hunting!

— *Matthew*

BLOOMS APLENTY

Lilacs are an edible flower, which makes them natural garnishes for salads, infused spirits, and baked goods, such as these cupcakes (opposite). Bake up your favorite recipe for cupcakes, or purchase a dozen from the bakery or grocery store. Topped with white frosting, the cupcakes show off the variety of lilac bloom colors, from white to deep purple. Lilacs also come in pink and burgundy, as well. You can make these adorable little swizzle sticks (this page) by inserting slender toothpicks into the ends of the blooms, and standing them up in jelly jars filled with fizzy white grape juice.

TIP To preserve lilac petals, check online for recipes for sugaring them, which turns them into crystallized, edible garnishes. The blogger ACanadianFoodie.com shares step-by-step photos. Or press the petals between paper towels and heavy books to flatten and dry them.

TIP Unlike hydrangeas, lilacs don't dry well as preserved flowers, so enjoy their gorgeous color and optimize their heady scent by hanging them near an open window.

FRESH MESSAGES OF LOVE

In the language of flowers, purple lilacs symbolize the first emotions of love, and white lilacs represent youthful innocence. Combine the two in a welcoming springtime bouquet that hangs on the front door (this page). By twining the stems and hanging them upside down, the flowers won't droop as they dry out. Dress a table with a fragrant but simple centerpiece arrangement of cut lilacs in purple glass bottles (opposite). The vessels need not be fancy—soda bottles with the labels removed will do.

WHISPER SWEET NOTHINGS Fashion one-of-a-kind pillows out of vintage lilac art. Scan the image from an art print, botanical book, or even an old greeting card, and enlarge it on your computer to the desired size. Print it on fabric transfer paper (above), which you can buy at the crafts store, and use an iron to transfer the design to a piece of linen fabric or a pillow cover. Linen allows the aroma of stress-reducing buckwheat-hull stuffing to permeate, making the pillow as hardworking as it is decorative (opposite).

TIP Fabric transfer paper comes in several sizes, but 8x11 inches and 11x17 inches are most common. It's also made for several kinds of printers, from inkjets to lasers, so know what you have before you shop.

FOREIGN EXCHANGE

Embracing her passion for European flea markets, collector and shop owner Jocie Sinauer shares her mastery of the art of displaying antiques.

MIX AND MATCH
The elegant details and furnishings in the dining room
(this page) of Jocie's home demonstrate her love of mixing
textures, patina, and provenance. To achieve this look,
search for pieces with a distressed finish and combine
different wood tones and paint hues. Jocie accessorizes with
elegant statement pieces like these ornate candlesticks and
her collection of heavyweight hotel silver (opposite).

EUROPEAN INFLUENCE

To create an air of casual elegance in her home, Jocie gravitates to a more modern approach to using antiques, keeping the emphasis on form, function, and patina. In the living room (this page), Jocie reupholstered her settee in 19th century French linen. You can achieve a similar look and feel by using unbleached cotton or a durable ticking fabric. A distressed Swedish cabinet (opposite) is filled with an eclectic flea market mix of creamware, pewter, sea shells, and coral.

1

2

WHEN YOU CROSS THE THRESHOLD of the home of Jocie Sinauer and her husband David Chicane, you instantly feel as though you've been swept across the Atlantic and welcomed into a sophisticated yet comfortable European farmhouse. Jocie, owner of Red Chair on Warren in Hudson, New York, fills her home with antiques gathered during her frequent trips to France and Belgium's finest flea markets. Her carefully curated and edited collections of silver, ironstone, time-worn furnishings, and organic offerings from nature speak to Jocie's well-known reputation as an educated and thoughtful collector. But as all serious collectors know, how each piece is displayed is just as important as its pedigree; thus Jocie seeks out the perfect vessels, cupboards, trestle tables and cabinets to serve as elegant backdrops to showcase her treasured finds. Jocie holds a special fondness for French linens, ephemera, and armoires, and when selecting a color palette for her home, was inspired by the silvery-grey hue of the Swedish furniture pieces that she seeks out on her trips abroad. It is this attention to detail that guides Jocie's choices when shopping for the exquisite antiques and collectibles that each of her favorite flea markets (near or far) is known for.

BEAUTY MULTIPLIED

The choice to start a particular collection often begins with that first, memorable purchase. As the collection grows, so does the impact it makes in your home. "Organized displays create harmony and balance, and inject a sense of calm to a larger grouping," says Jocie. Whether displayed in twos or as part of a larger group, each piece complements the other and ups the wow factor of a vignette. **1.** A pair of shells, found at a flea market, rest on a salvaged newel post. **2.** A collection of vintage mercury glass sparkles below an antique mirror and are an example of Jocie's panache for grouping like objects with dramatic effect. **OPPOSITE:** Weathered urns filled with fresh greenery sit atop an antique pine table. Below, a vintage sink basin adds an unexpected element to the display. Follow your instincts, not a set of rules, suggests Jocie. "If you live by rules, you rule things out," she says. "Be open to fresh ideas."

TIP: Don't be afraid to mix old and new. Search flea markets for authentic vintage finds and fill in the blanks with vintage-inspired and reproduction pieces.

SHADES OF LIGHT

Jocie punctuates a distressed table with two matching chairs and a giant piece of coral. A sheepskin rug adds softness underfoot, and a vintage milk glass pendant hangs above. Matching vintage mirrors flank the dining space. OPPOSITE: Vintage apothecary jars filled with beach stones, shells, and goose eggs reflect Jocie's love of collecting and displaying organic materials, purchased at flea markets and auctions.

GOT MILK

You don't have to look far to find inexpensive milk glass to accent your home. Design blogger Layla Palmer shows you just how easy it is to give your home its "daily allowance."

TIP: Authentic milk glass can date as far back as the 18th century. Consider joining a milk glass society to help you identify the age and origin of your collection.

OFF THE SHELF A grouping of milk glass commands attention when displayed against a colorful background. Layla injects modernity to a tried and true display method by hanging milk glass plates on a boldly colored wall (above). Juxtaposed with a mid-century chair, their graphic shapes and patterns help pull off a look that is decidedly updated. A vintage metal rubber-stamp holder (opposite) corrals personalized coffee creamers and toothpick holders filled with spring buds. For Easter, Layla fills some of the little cups with tiny chocolate eggs and places them on her holiday table.

ASK DESIGN BLOGGER, PHOTO STYLIST, and DIY maven **Layla Palmer** what she loves about milk glass and her response is as enthusiastic as her approach to cottage style, which she chronicles on her popular blog, TheLetteredCottage.net. "Milk glass is the perfect blend of found and fresh," says Layla, "because every piece has a wonderful sense of history, but continues to stand out in interiors today." And because reproduction pieces can be found at flea markets, yard sales, and thrift shops for as little as 50 cents, milk glass is the perfect collectible for beginners who are looking to acquire items that can be used without fretting about breakage. Indeed, milk glass—commonly used as flower vessels in the 1960s and 1970s by florists—goes beyond the usefulness of just filling up shelves or cupboards for display. Pieces can be grouped together for decorative impact, but then used individually for entertaining, floral arrangements, or whatever unique interpretation Layla has up her sleeve on any given day. Known for thinking outside the box, Layla shares some of her imaginative but easy ideas for putting this wholesome collection to good use.

THE MILKY WAY Milk glass comes in a variety of simple shapes and styles but can also boast rather intricate patterns, fluting, and cut-outs (above left). Layla (above right) suggests playing up its trademark white against a bold or patterned backdrop: "It's an easy way to add a contemporary feel."
OPPOSITE: 1. These milk glass baking cups came with plastic lids for storing. Set them on a desk caddy for organizing office essentials and label with a sticker. **2.** A small bottle becomes a cheery posy holder. Simply wrap the neck with ribbon, personalize with letter decals, and hang on a pretty hook. **3.** Look for cake stands and compotes of different sizes and detailing. Layla uses hers to display other small collections or to elevate a treasured object. **4.** A tiny milk glass pot becomes a pin cushion with a scrap of fabric and some hollow fill.

5

clips

1

2

1

lettered COTTAGE

2

3

4

1   2

3   4

STAND AND DELIVER Displayed in groupings (this page), milk glass delivers a healthy dose of style.
OPPOSITE: 1. Layla plants compotes and serving cups with slips of her favorite plants. **2.** Many collectors look for multi-textured pieces with decorative patterns which predate their floral shop cousins and are more coveted: a quality their price reflects. **3.** Layla stacks graduated cake stands atop one another for interest. She loads them up with cupcakes or treats for special occasions. **4.** An early rolling pin, missing its handles, is reborn as a lamp using a simple wiring kit from a hardware store.

COOL DOODLE

Graphic, bold, and personal, doodle art is not just a way to endure a boring meeting, it can lead to inspired decorating projects, too.

WIN, LOSE, OR DRAW
Several years ago at a flea market, Matthew found a tattered art book featuring hundreds of black-and-white doodles. The unscripted, looping lines inspired him to unroll an industrial-size spool of craft paper and scrawl happily with a Sharpie® marker (opposite). The result, when hung with chains and S-hooks from picture molding, is a fetching bit of "art" for the living room wall. Other canvases for ever-changing scrawls are pizza pans coated in chalkboard paint (this page).

LARGER THAN LIFE

Scan black-and-white art sketches or your own doodles and enlarge them to bold proportions. Upload them to a copy store web site, such as FedEx® Office, to have them printed on large paper. Spooled inside a glass cylinder lamp (this page), or pasted to home-center closet-door panels using découpage medium (opposite), they are appealing conversation-starters.

IT'S BLACK OR WHITE

Cluster decorative objects to underscore the graphic nature of doodles. A vintage cookbook is open to the title page, showing its modern design. A piece of slate is an old-fashioned canvas for chalk scribbles. And baling wire, found at a flea market of farm wares, is coaxed into script and tacked to the wall.

ARTFUL PIN-UPS
Flea-market bins full of old
correspondence and ephemera are
gold mines of doodle art. Tack up
sketches, notes, and cards you find
appealing to inspiration boards, such
as this piece of sheet metal.

ON A BENDER

Pliable baling wire might not seem like a treasure at first, but Matthew spied its potential for wire creations and snatched it up at a farm sale. **1.** This coil of old wire cost just $2. Used for a variety of farm chores, from repairing fences to wrapping hay bundles, new baling wire is available by the foot at farm surplus stores and hardware stores, but it will cost much more. **2.** Use wire cutters and needle-nose pliers to bend the wire into curlicues and loops. Always wear gloves to protect your hands. **3.** Just as rustic as wire, this river rock is a paperweight or decorative object when you add chalk stripes. Wash it clean and start again when you get bored with the design. **OPPOSITE:** Matthew had fun imitating scrawling doodles to fashion these wire frames for old family photos. You can follow his lead by downloading the patterns at HolidayWithMatthewMead.com, or just have fun twisting your own.

STICK AROUND

By enlarging copies of drawings in his vintage art book, Matthew perked up two plain side chairs (opposite). The square chairs suit the doodles and make papering easy. Using a straightedge and Xacto® knife, cut paper sections to fit the seats, backs, and aprons of the chairs. Brush a portion of a chair with découpage medium (we like ModPodge®) and smooth on a piece of paper, using the straightedge if needed. Seal the surface with a second coat of ModPodge. For a tilt-top table (this page), he similarly découpaged a sketch of a chandelier to the top, then traced a border design using black permanent marker.

PAPER PARADE

Depending on the style of the artist, these doodles can feel contemporary or classic. "I like all styles," Matthew says. "I just try to match the doodle to the project."

OPPOSITE: Single blooms in an urn-style vase have a traditional feel, so Matthew chose to apply the designs to a charming old jewelry dresser. **1.** The piece's flat surfaces—inside the door panels and across the façade—make for easy découpage. Brush on the glue-like medium using a clean paintbrush, and then position the papers. The medium dries clear, so you can use it as a sealant as well. **2.** For this abstract maze-like illustration, Matthew created a mod sculpture using wood blocks purchased at a flea market. The blocks were likely used individually to display pottery in a gallery, but when stacked, they work together to show off the enlarged illustration. Measure the assembled boxes, and then scan, expand, and print the doodle to fit. Cut it in sections for each box, and adhere with découpage medium. **3.** Inside books that were published in the middle of the 20th century, you'll find graphic design indicative of the period. Use them as fodder for your projects.

CHILD'S PLAY

Take a peek inside a magical playhouse where old meets new and little girls' dreams are played out in fanciful detail using a collection of flea market treasures.

ENTER IN
Pretty shades of yellow, pink, and blue beckon small visitors to this pint-sized garden getaway (opposite). Whimsical details – like the vintage mailbox and doll carriage – appeal to guests of all ages. Decorate a child's space easily with cheerful finds from the flea market. Stacks of vintage dishware (above) are ready to be used for an impromptu tea party with a friend.

A BOUQUET OF COLOR

Florals and pastels, set against a backdrop of white, inject the tiny space with color and pattern (opposite). Mismatched vintage sheets – in shades of pink, yellow, and orange – dress the daybed and were a happy find at a yard sale. Wire baskets can be used to store favorite books for an afternoon of quiet reading. Small floral cuttings from a nearby flower garden fill old containers and dishes, while a platter filled with gumballs offers a sugary treat for all who visit.

IT'S ALL IN THE DETAILS

1. Numbered acrylic glasses add colorful order to a space reserved strictly for fun. Below them, the playhouse's small window sports a lightweight café curtain hung using a simple tree branch.

2. A pair of whimsical wooden hangers—vintage thrift shop finds—hangs cheerily on the wall. Scour flea markets for vintage children's items to bring age-appropriate appeal to a play space.

3. Child-sized vintage aprons can often be found for several dollars and are a fun collection to begin as a child. Display them together for a pretty effect or bring them inside for a day of baking or imaginative play.

4. A winsome porcelain pup—crowned in a flowery cap—charms from his perch up high on a shelf. Porcelain animals are highly collectible and hold special appeal to children.

5. Vintage tea towels and table linens are common finds at tag sales and flea markets. Look for embroidered items that are free of damage and hang them on a wall or row of hooks for a charming show of color and pattern.

6. A built-in daybed layered with vintage bedding and plump pillows offers a perfect spot for an afternoon nap. Timeworn linens benefit from years of laundering which leaves them wonderfully soft and with pretty, muted colors. Those with small holes or imperfections) are often overlooked and can be purchased for a song and used as fabric for smaller projects.

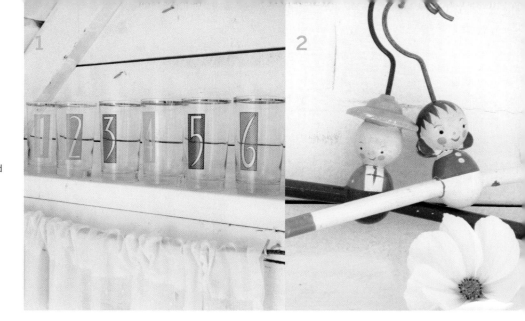

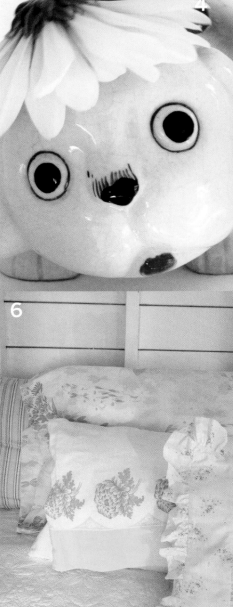

CHERISHED WHATNOTS

Small treasures like this pink-striped Carrigaline pitcher, vintage children's book, and skeleton key (this page) tell the story of what the owner of this adorable little playhouse loves to collect. Packets of heritage sweet pea seeds await planting and rest atop a shelf trimmed with a patterned vintage pillowcase. To avoid damaging the fabric, use adhesive-backed hook and loop tape to secure vintage linens to surfaces. Children are natural collectors and love to show off their finds – like these vintage aprons (opposite) hanging from a line.

HERITAGE
SWEET PEAS
OLD SPICE MIX
3.5G

VINTAGE HEIRLOOM VA

CHAS. C. HART S
WETHERSFIELD

"Little girls love tea parties, and with parents as guests, bringing out the vintage dishware is not such a reckless notion." — *Matthew*

A POCKET-FULL OF POSIES

A vintage teapot, embossed with daisies (opposite), is filled with cold lemonade for a child-friendly tea party refreshment. Retro plastic tumblers await filling with the lemony beverage and can be found for a bargain at yard sales, thrift shops and tag sales. Melmac plastic dishes are the perfect choice when looking for colorful yet unbreakable dishes for children's play and use. Hand-wash all vintage dishes and glassware to preserve their condition and prevent cracking or breakage.

TEA FOR TWO

1. Loaded up with berry-filled tarts, tea cakes, and meringues, a vintage tiered platter heaves under the load of its sugary confection.

2. Topped off with an icy drink of lemonade "tea," the biggest decision these guests (and girls) will have to make is when to stop nibbling!

3. A bowlful of sweet Rainier cherries awaits eager guests and offer a healthy alternative to all of the sugary sweetness.

4. A large yellow glass jar from the flea market does double duty as a serving vessel when filled with ice water and lemon slices. Use a ladle to serve up the cold drink.

5. One is never enough when the cookies are this good. When decorating cookies for a tea party, draw inspiration from the patterns on the vintage dishes and glassware.

6. A collection of vintage bowls, glass plates, and cake stands are used to serve up a bevy of delicious treats. Blueberry and strawberry tarts – topped with fresh cream – compete with fresh, juicy strawberries for the party-goers attention. When using vintage dishes, layer pieces on top of one another for added interest and color. Dress party tables with vintage table cloths and placemats to infuse nostalgic appeal and charm, and to serve as a colorful backdrop for the tempting array of sweet desserts.

OLD MEETS NEW Until the baby arrives, the spotlight is on the nursery's vintage china cupboard (opposite) and cheery aqua crib. Both received a makeover with fresh paint and stylish accessories (see page 158 for paint colors). Stephanie chose vintage inspired artwork (this page) from AllPosters.com and slipped them into gilded custom frames.

BABY STEPS

Stephanie Nielson reveals her nesting instinct and unveils the vintage inspired nursery of her much anticipated baby girl.

Last fall, when **Stephanie Nielson** revealed on her popular blog (NieNieDialogues.com) that she was expecting her fifth child in April, her readers rejoiced with her. As a survivor of a near-fatal airplane crash in 2008, Stephanie's ability to safely have more children was initially in question. "There have been plenty of miracles surrounding my accident; I've seen them first-hand," Stephanie says. "This baby is my favorite miracle of all and we're so excited for her to join our family!" And with the construction of a new family home also in the works, the Nielsons chose a nursery design that can be carried over to the new home when it's ready. Stephanie and Christian collaborated with Matthew Mead to create a vintage-inspired oasis that is the perfect blend of old meets new. "Everything Matthew creates is beautiful," says Stephanie, "and his use of colorful accessories fits my desire to keep the walls white and add in color with all of the charming details. I love the nursery design so much that I plan to just transfer everything to my new home, and then have fun choosing wallpaper, lighting, and window treatments."

STORYBOOK DETAILS Besides welcoming a new baby and building a house, 2012 will also see the release (inset, left) of Stephanie's book, Heaven is Here (2011; Hyperion Publishing), which is available though Amazon.com. It's the story of the miracle of her survival and recovery, and the hope and faith she clung to as she rebuilt her life. The nesting process begins: **1.** Claire, 10, holds up a treasured baby sweater **2.** Nicholas, 5, admires his mother's growing belly **3.** Oliver, 7, peeks out over a pillow made using fabric from Warm Biscuit Bedding Co. (see page 158 for pattern info). **4.** Stephanie had the change table painted in the same color as the crib, then stored baby supplies in vintage wicker baskets. **5.** The back of the wardrobe received a wallpaper treatment in the pillow fabric pattern. Stuffed toys, vintage children's books, and pretty dresses are ready for use. **6.** Jane, 9, helps decorate the nursery.

3

4

5

6

CRIB NOTES: When refinishing nursery furniture, use low VOC latex paint in a color that will grow with your baby, and allow it to cure before placing it in the room.

WELL-STOCKED

Matthew purchased this over-sized cabinet (opposite) at a New Hampshire flea market and had it shipped to Stephanie to provide attractive storage in a room that needed it. "I don't have much space in this room to store my baby items," Stephanie says. "So when Matthew suggested that I use the wardrobe, I knew it would be the perfect solution to my storage woes." Matthew revived it with a new coat of paint, crystal knobs, and vintage details. A rug (in Lighthouse Khaki from Dash and Albert) is layered over the room's carpet. Special thanks to Jessica Bennett and her team at Alice Lane (AliceLaneHome.com) for furnishings logistics.

VINTAGE BABY

1. 1.Nicholas gets silly with a giant stuffed owl, one of Stephanie's favorite themes.
2. A vintage card holder displays old postcards Stephanie has collected since childhood.
3. Stephanie loves this ceramic owl from Etsy.com. "I love owls; they are delicate and sweet and perfect for a baby's room."
4. Christian, aka "Mr. Nielson," holds a tiny pair of pink booties—sweet hand-me-downs from Claire and Jane.
5. Matthew found this spinning photo holder at a flea market and filled it with pages from a vintage bird book.
6. Flea markets are the perfect place to find whimsical items for a nursery. Stephanie loves the intricate bird carvings of this vintage wooden plate and propped it on one of the wardrobe's shelves. "Since I will spend a lot of time in this nursery, too, I decided to choose colors and themes that I find soothing and beautiful," she says.

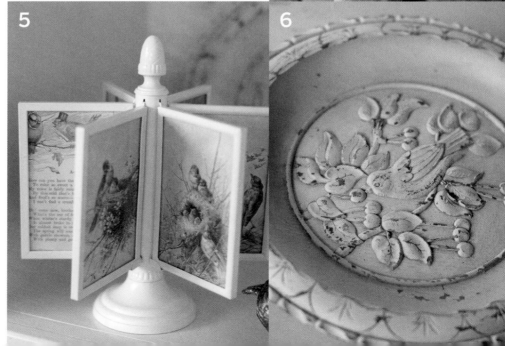

MID-CENTURY MATTHEW

He has always been hip to collect Modern furniture and accessories, and here he shares how these chic, streamlined pieces can find a groove in your home.

THOROUGHLY MODERN

The colors of the mid-Century era are back in fashion today. To introduce them on a small scale, look for accessories, such as this speckled stoneware vase from Glidden Pottery (this page). So many similar wares were produced in the 1940s and '50s, they're still affordable today—Matthew spent just $8 for his. To furnish a comfortable seating area for visitors to his studio (opposite), Matthew turned to secondhand Modern pieces and spent less than $300 for everything. The print above the sofa is a vintage Volkswagen magazine ad that he scanned, enlarged, and printed at a copy store.

1   **2**

3

JUICY COUTURE

A color borrowed from all-the-rage Pop Art, orange continues to make a splash in home interiors. **1.** Two ceramic pieces by prolific companies Glidden and McCoy are put to use on a laminate bureau. Shiny chrome offset by organic wood was a popular combo indicative of contemporary style. This lamp base shows the pairing in a graphic stack of blocks and circles. **2.** To perk up this $50 wood-and-metal side chair, Matthew recovered the cushions in tight brown linen. The new orange sofa pillows are fresh imports from a flea market vendor Matthew sought out. **3.** Create your own mix of earthy and metallic elements with an aluminum trophy plate filled with metal carpet balls and walnuts. **OPPOSITE:** "My favorite finds lately are these sleek interpretations of Windsor-style chairs," Matthew says. Bought for $70, the pair merges with an old office chair and a stool to make a conversation grouping around a cork cooler used as a coffee table. A vintage black floor lamp ($25) sheds some light.

KITCHEN LABORATORY

Truly a hardworking space, the kitchen in Matthew's studio is where he and his team of creative cooks churn out the recipes for which he is known. It's also where he stages and prepares the food he photographs for Associated Press articles. "This kitchen needs to be easy and breezy," he says. To achieve that goal, Matthew relies on Modern elements, which are inherently low-fuss and suited to mixing and matching.

METALLURGES

Restaurants may come and go, but their kitchen fittings last forever. Matthew scours flea markets for stainless and aluminum tables, chairs, stools, and even pots and pans leftover from these hardworking spaces. A few scratches and nicks from previous owners keep the prices low, but they just meld with the efforts of Matthew's crew. The console table and the square island cost just $50 apiece.

STORE MORE

When it comes to storage in a kitchen, bigger is always better. Which is why Matthew seized a locker that once resided in a post office to install in his kitchen. At $200, the flea-market find was not a steal, but it has proved its industrial mettle holding weighty stacks of dishes. Matthew looks for other large vessels, such as stoneware bowls and glass canisters from science labs, to use for bulk items.

SIMPLY WHITE

Maintaining multiple sets of patterned dishware would be difficult and costly when inevitable breakage occurs in the kitchen. Instead, Matthew relies on plain white pieces from every era, any source, and all makers to work together. "We accumulate them from all over, and use them to make as well as serve food," he says.

INTERESTING FINDS

There's always room in Matthew and Jenny's trunk for a random extra find at any flea market or estate sale they attend. It's space reserved for the item they couldn't have foreseen, such as the 80-pound marble slab now kept on the kitchen island. It likely came from a European chocolate or cheese store, and may have been used to display delectables at a consistent temperature. The stone keeps food cool, which is invaluable under hot photography lights.

STAND-INS

A favorite collectible from any era—mid-Century or not—is the cake stand. It can be employed to display a cake, of course, but Matthew has found that the pedestals give nearly anything else, from Christmas ornaments to office supplies, an elegant look. He keeps the kitchen stocked with several at all times.

FLASHES OF BRILLIANCE

Two iconic items from the Modern era give the kitchen its fun personality: the bold wall clock and the molded plastic pendant light.

"Having kitchen tools within reach or quickly accessible makes the work much easier." — *Matthew*

TIP: To keep metal surfaces streak-free, Matthew uses a soft, dry cloth to wipe them down with WD-40. Don't use it on food prep areas, such as tabletops, however.

"I love Modern spaces because they are open and light. They're casual enough for easy entertaining, and usually have a jolt of energizing color."

— *Matthew*

HAVING FUN AT LOW COST

What others find frustrating about flea market shopping, Matthew finds tantalizing and joyful: You never know what you're going to find. You have to dig around to unearth a treasure, and it may not even be a treasure at all until you give it a good cleaning. But the effort is reflected in the price tags. Unless you're looking for the same thing everyone else is, therefore driving up prices, you're paying a little bit for something that's quirky and interesting. "That's something you can't say about your typical mall experience," Matthew says.

WHY FUN MATTERS

1. You can enjoy a chuckle. "People get a laugh when I open the locker door and give them an impromptu eye exam," Matthew says of this vintage eye chart he hangs inside the locker/pantry.

2. You can see things in new ways. This locker stored coats and galoshes, but Matthew fitted it with extra-thick glass shelves so he could store his glassware and dinnerware inside.

3. You'll be healthier. Flea markets are set up on sprawling tracks of land under the blue sky. You'll fill up on fresh air and walk miles up and down the aisles looking for the next best thing at a vendor's stand, such as this extra large chemistry beaker Matthew uses as a fruit bowl.

4. You'll hone your home improvement skills. When you shop at flea markets, you'll rarely find anything in mint condition. The frame of this wall clock was chipped and a bit rusty, so Matthew cleaned it, sanded off the rust, and gave it a new coat of paint.

5. Your style will be unique. Bringing home one-of-a-kind finds from estate sales and thrift stores makes you appreciate the work of artisans, too. "Jenny shops Etsy.com for creative accessories like this teapot to give our rooms a kick," Matthew says.

6. You'll learn patience. Flea market shopping forces you to slow down and let things evolve naturally. You can't build an entire collection of orange pottery in one afternoon, but you can start with a smashing, futuristic salt-and-pepper combo.

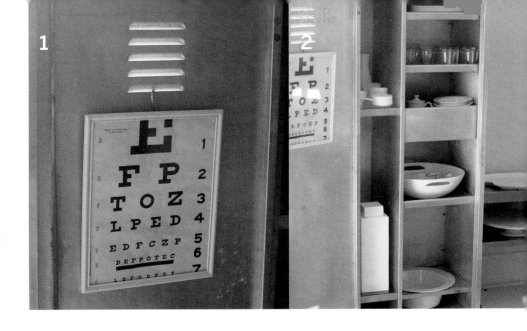

1 **2**

3

CREATIVE FUEL
This pint-sized office spot is just right for Matthew to plunk down with his iPad to search for Pinterest inspiration during lulls in a photo shoot. **OPPOSITE:** The table is a rolling metal trolley, and the chairs came from a sale of out-of-date office furniture. For $25 each, he could afford to have them recovered in grainy gray fabric. The penguin-shape lamp ($75) already had a comical appearance, and Matthew added to it with an "@" symbol vinyl decal ordered online. **1.** Vintage cameras, flashes, and old photos always catch Matthew's eye at thrift stores. The equipment doesn't have to work. It's just a reminder of an art that's personally meaningful. **2.** Cork trivets are tactile inspiration boards. "You don't have to hang them on the wall, just lean them up against something," Matthew says.
3. Admitting a weakness for pottery and glass pieces, Matthew has amassed a collection that spreads beyond the studio and into his and Jenny's home. When he gets bored of a piece or a color, he switches them out. Thankfully, they are not costly items: The combined price of these three gold objects was only $30.

GARDEN CHARM

Decorate your home, porch,
or retreat space with the timeworn
appeal of cottage style using
the comfy look and aged patina
of flea market finds.

MADE TO ORDER COLOR

Vintage finds help turn this garden shed into a cottage-style retreat. A wrought-iron soap holder holds a cold cream jar used as a vase (opposite). The homeowner chose a color palette inspired by sea glass collected during her family's trips to the Maine coast. To furnish the space, Matthew sought out pottery in watery bluesand greens, and gave a few wood pieces, such as the settee, a color wash to coordinate (this page).

1   **2**

3

"This garden shed was used to store extra pots and supplies. Now, with a good scrubbing and some furnishings, it's a restorative afternoon retreat." — *Matthew*

METHOD TO THE MAKEOVER

To transform this space from a rough shed to a cozy getaway, Matthew relied on flea market shopping to find equally rustic furnishings that suited the homeowner's small budget. **1.** Pots and trugs indicate the shed's first purpose. These implements now reside on shelves in the garage. **2.** A metal waste can (probably from a business office) shows off some of the lush Hosta leaves growing outside. Matthew gave the can a spray of blue paint. **3.** Painted-metal grain bins serve as handy trays for ferrying drinks or cut flowers to and from the kitchen. **OPPOSITE:** Not everyone has a garden shed like this that's worth claiming as a personal retreat. Consider a cottagey makeover for your porch or home office. Or, simply set up a seating area under a tree in the yard.

THE LIVIN' IS EASY

The shed's effortless décor comes from simple displays such as this. Snippets of tall grasses fill out a McCoy vase, and honed beach glass shards that were collected over many years reside in a canning jar. If you don't have access to the seashore, you can purchase beach glass by the pound online and in crafts stores. A primitive cupboard wears a coat of turquoise paint (opposite). To give wood furniture an aged look, Matthew mixes equal parts water and latex paint, brushes it on lightly, and then wipes much of it off with a dry rag.

"This space is open to the
weather, so we didn't pick
any precious furnishings.
Everything here can stand a
little more wear-and-tear."
— *Matthew*

1

2

3

TELL A STORY

The look of this retreat started with the homeowner's love of the seashore. Matthew drew upon the hues of the water and her beach glass collection to pick furnishings. Then, he filled out the space with mementoes that provide comfort and inspiration. **1.** Matthew found this stool, which performs as a side table, snack tray, and as extra seating, in a refreshing aqua color at a flea market. **2.** This antique lantern comes in handy during the evening hours and on dark rainy days. **3.** A smattering of shells fills a shallow pottery crock. **OPPOSITE:** The homeowner is an avid gardener, and she comes out to the shed to plan and sketch the gardens. For more restful afternoons, Matthew set up a daybed on what was once the potting bench, using an upholstered foam cushion and several pillows. A Sunday painting from a flea market in Maine gives the shed a sea view.

To display the homeowner's collection of sea-smoothed beach glass, Matthew sprinkled them into vintage seed-starting tins (this page) and set them on a table. Other antiques culled from flea markets, estate sales, and thrift stores give the shed its cottagey charm (opposite). A wooden bandbox painted blue stands as a side table to a French settee. Rather than reupholster the torn seat, Matthew just placed a folded piece of linen over the cushion. No longer in working order, a metal fan has a sculptural look on a tramp-art pedestal covered in tiny seashells.

"Personal retreats should be just that—
personal. Whatever makes you happy will
be at home in these spaces." — *Matthew*

FROND MOMENTS

Though rooted in
the Victorian era, the
appealing simplicity
of fern collectibles
makes them graceful
accents for today's
homes and gardens.

THE FRIENDLY FERN Quietly undemanding, ferns ask little from the garden apart from shade and moisture, and offer composed symmetry and luscious shades of green that suggest health and vitality (opposite). It's no wonder the nature-loving Victorians featured them in artistic and intellectual pursuits, from hand-painted china to botanical illustrations. Flea markets are flush with such ephemera, and it's easy to use the bounty in new ways. For a touch of spring in your home, display aged pages from a plant book in clear apothecary jars (above), which are inexpensive finds without lids.

TURN THE PAGE

There is a plethora of fern illustrations to use in decorative projects. Mine flea market booths for old gardening books or botany texts. **1.** Make a color-copy of a fern print and adhere it to the bottom of a glass trivet using decoupage medium, such as ModPodge®. **2.** Flea market vendors sell single-page sketches and prints such as these in protective vellum sleeves. You can buy just a few to copy again and again. **3.** Part plant identifier and part travel guide, this vintage book, which was originally copyrighted in 1899, provides descriptions and illustrations of the author's fern finds. The decorative cover makes it easy to display on its own, or browse the advice inside to find live specimens locally. **OPPOSITE:** Once used to post bills and signs around town, this display box has renewed charm thanks to a coat of white paint and a stenciled label. Enlarge a botanical image to fit inside.

ferns

VIEWED BEHIND GLASS

Whether you snip them from a plant in your shady backyard or a pot on the dining room sideboard, fern fronds are just as striking in single-stem vases as big, feathery clusters. **1.** Delicate baby fern fronds are delightful captured in the smooth bubble of a translucent rose bowl. Look for rose bowl collectibles, which are indoor garden display cases that hark back to the Victorian fascination with single roses, and use the lid to corral a bit of soil for the plant roots. Once sealed, the mini-terrarium will water itself. **2.** For a terrarium anyone can create—regardless of your green thumb—insert a gently coiled botanical print into the narrow mouth of a giant vase, vintage bottle, or apothecary jar. **3.** Green glass bottles are tidy vessels for a variety of fern fronds. **OPPOSITE:** Cluster the bottles together to create a centerpiece for a picnic table nestled into a wooded setting. Snip the fronds nearby, and then set the table with a mixture of newly crafted and vintage patterned dinnerware.

STACK THE PLATES

"Fern collectibles become part of your lifestyle," says Matthew, who fell in love with a set of turn-of-the-century fern-pattern china a decade ago. "Taking a walk, I notice ferns everywhere now." **1.** Thanks to simple colors and patterns, china with fern decorations—such as this single teapot, a recent flea-market find—mix and match easily with pieces from all eras. **2.** Grace a table setting with snippets of live ferns, which are hardy enough to hold their color and shape without water for several hours. **3.** Haven't found a vintage place setting yet? Make one by copying fern illustrations and decoupaging them to the underside of plain glass plates. These square dessert plates are a modern touch.

OPPOSITE: Look for glass plates at secondhand stores, and adhere the illustrations to the bottom. For a bold look, enlarge the image to several times its original size and place it off-center. When the meal is over, skip the dishwasher and hand-wash the plates.

THE REAL DEAL

Ferns are shade-loving perennials that quickly reproduce. They thrive in wild thickets, in carefully tended plots, and even as houseplants. Gather some fronds while on a hike, and bring them home to display live or press and dry. **1.** The central stem and symmetrical leaves of a stout fern were a pleasing subject for the carver who made this rectangular tray Matthew unearthed at a yard sale. **2.** Lay a few fronds on napkins to perk up a place setting. **3.** Showcase the spectacular fan shape and delicate airiness of this maidenhead fern by putting one singular stem in an antique green glass bottle. **OPPOSITE:** A quick, easy, and appealing centerpiece, fill the buckets of a vintage muffin tin with water and tiny fern snippets. To set off their verdant colors, first spray the tin with a coat of matte white paint, and distress it with sandpaper if desired.

NATURE'S ARTISTRY Replicate the beauty of these plants using paint and stencils, and you'll enjoy them evermore. Look for stencils at crafts stores and online sites, and choose large ones to create impact. Using stencil adhesive, apply the stencils to a wall or the front of a flat piece of furniture, such as this down-on-its-luck secretary (opposite), and fill in with paint in various shades of green. When the leaves are dry, go back and paint on thin stems and veins (above), and then seal and protect the entire motif by spraying or brushing on a coat of clear polyurethane.

INDUSTRIAL REVOLUTION

Create signature style by employing functional relics left over from factories, office buildings, and the retail floor.

Grow

PROJECTIONS FOR GROWTH

Top a metal trestle table with an iron heating grate and pull up a vintage lab stool to create a handy spot for indoor gardening and orchid growing. A wall covered in chalkboard paint keeps notes and watering schedules in view, and a wheeled custodial bucket serves as a planter. Propped in back, a sectioned wooden crate divider serves as an impromptu lattice support for the delicate stems of the orchids.

ORCHIDS
water every monday

FACTORY NEW Salvaged from a leather-punching factory, this metal desk has seen its share of use (opposite). Give it a gentler purpose as a correspondence center, filling the drawers with stationery and letterpress supplies. Pull up a chair from a shoe-stitching factory, which has adjustable heights for different workers. A time-card rack secured to the jonquil-yellow wall shows off vintage papers, colorful plates, and mementoes. On the floor, an aluminum radio case (above) holds extra scrapbooking tools and papers.

TABLE FOR TWO A municipal trash can gets a bistro-style makeover when it's topped with a circle of shatterproof glass (above). Use double-stick rubber cushions to hold the glass in place. Where the town insignia once resided, spell out a catchphrase in adhesive address letters purchased at the hardware store. Pull up a couple of stools, and illuminate the scene with a glass chemistry funnel threaded over a funky pendant light. A labeled factory tray becomes graphic wall art.

BATHING BEAUTIES

Wheeled carts are particularly versatile. This tall wire stand from a glass factory provides extra storage for pretty bath essentials. A zinc-topped cobbler's table performs as a stool at the vanity, which was once a commercial sewing table, or can roll tubside to offer up lotions and salts. Turn a piece of sheet metal into wall art by stenciling on letters in crafts paint.

B A T H

RIBBON

HARD WORK PAYS OFF

The first piece of vintage industrial equipment Matthew purchased at a flea market was this rugged metal trolley. "I'm always excited about items that have wheels," he says. It moves from room to room as needed to house electronics, corral crafts supplies, or display collectibles. "Factory wares were designed to hold up to lots of wear and tear, so they were solidly built," he says. "This trolley has presence."

ELEMENTS OF THE LOOK

1. Boxes and baskets keep open shelves tidy by storing wrapping papers and ribbons. "I like to keep these items handy for when I need to quickly wrap up a hostess gift," Matthew says. "But I don't want them unraveling and spilling everywhere."

2. Stacks of rustic gear with the same hardy appearance of the cart—such as these old wood molds for soaps, candy, and candles—make for an interesting display.

3. A lamp without its shade has the right utilitarian look. Shop for old-fashioned-style clear bulbs, such as this carbon filament bulb from Rejuvenation.com, to complete the look. A factory-size metal fan shield is a striking decorative accessory.

4. Packaging supplies and string hide out in a long red-painted box, which was once used to mold bars of soap.

5. Manuals outlining rigid factory policies and procedures are fun to look through, and they are a tongue-in-cheek foil for the serene Buddhist icon.

6. There's room for beauty on the functional cart, as well. Matthew mixes in a metal fish sculpture and a vintage jar full of polished river stones.

FIT TO BE DYED

Move over commercial color: Transform vintage
fabrics, textiles, and clothing into new-to-you
originals with easy dyeing techniques
using the personalized hues you adore.

ART WITH A PURPOSE

Take a nod from the past and bring new life to tired and faded linens. THIS PAGE: Vintage fabrics are hand-dipped in a sampling of colors until the desired hue is achieved. OPPOSITE: Trims and sewing notions can be dyed and used to dress up flea market finds.

TIPS AND TRICKS
Linen napkins, found at a thrift shop and hand-dyed in a variety of hues, offer an affordable way to customize a table setting. Read the fabric label before dyeing, as not all fabrics will accept dye. They include: those with 50% or more polyester content, bleach damage, a label reading Dry-Clean Only, or fabrics lined with a rubber backing or a water-repellent finish. If in doubt, test a swatch of the fabric first.

Paint is not the only way to revitalize vintage furniture. A simple stitched slip-cover, made using dyed fabrics, brings softness and color to this mid-century modern side table.

1

2

3

4

5

6

7

8

DYEING FOR COLOR

1. Dye samples rest in a collection of vintage glass test-tubes
2. Choose a palette and experiment using old fabric scraps.
3. Color dyeing is not for the purist: The final shade is often a happy surprise, and calls for an open mind. **4.** Before dyeing, begin with clean, dust-free items to ensure even coloring. **5.** Dyed cotton-twill tape can be used to trim gifts or the edges of shelves. **6.** Layers of dyed fabric offer a colorful backdrop for some favorite flea market finds.
7. A tired cotton shirt becomes fashion-forward with an infusion of lilac dye. **8.** A tidy stack of linens shows the many color intensities which can be achieved by using different shades or by soaking in the dye for longer.

"Dyeing fabrics is an organic color experience; there are no guarantees to the final shade created. Be open to the serendipitous nature of it and enjoy the surprise." — *Matthew Mead*

A RAINBOW OF COLOR
An array of brilliant or subtle color choices await you in the form of natural and man-made dyes. Companies like Dharma Trading Company (DharmaTrading.com) offer a number of fiber-reactive dyes that won't fade or run when laundered—perfect for updating thrift-store fashion finds.

Dyeing is a simple and satisfying artistic process. Decide on a palette and combine fabric, dye, soda ash, salt, and water to create colorful living.

FIND IT Scour flea markets, tag sales, and thrift shops for timeworn fabrics and trims that can be given new life with a color bath.

THINK OUTSIDE THE (DYE) BOX

More than just fabric can be given a shot of color. Woven sea grass, string, and even twine can be dipped in dye to dress up gifts, packages, and for use in craft projects. Keep in mind that every material accepts dye differently and with varying degrees of intensity. Remember to always wear gloves when dyeing and avoid using a plastic or fibreglass container, or you will end up with color where it was not intended!

COLORFUL HISTORY

Highlight a collection of old photographs (they can be found for under a dollar at antique shops and tag sales) in colorful fabric-covered frames.

YOU WILL NEED:
> Mat-board photo frames in assorted sizes.
> Dyed vintage fabric
> Fabric glue
> Sponge brush
> Scissors and craft knife
> Hot glue gun
> Vintage photographs
> (or photocopies of the originals)

1. Using scissors, cut fabric slightly larger than each frame.
2. Apply fabric glue to the front of the frame using a sponge brush.
3. Using the craft knife, cut an X slit in the center of the fabric.
4. Lay the frame face down onto the back of the fabric, centering the x slit with the photo opening.
5. Smooth the fabric onto the frame, pulling it taut from each corner.
6. Turn frame over and snip the fabric in the frame's opening from corner to corner, folding it back to reveal the photo opening. Smooth out any wrinkles and adhere all trimmed excess fabric to the back of the frame using hot glue.

HAVE A BALL

Download the template from HolidayWithMatthewMead.com to create this fun beach ball pillow for summertime picnics.

YOU WILL NEED:
> Two colors of dyed vintage fabric
> (use ½ yard of each color/ball).
> Straight pins and scissors
> Sewing machine, needle, and thread
> One bag of pillow stuffing
> Fabric covered buttons, made using scraps of the
> dyed fabric and hot glue.

1. Using the template, trace the shape onto the eight fabric pieces (four of each color). Cut each shape out. With their right sides facing in, pin two shapes (use both colors/pair) together, carefully lining up each point and edge. Repeat until you have four pinned pairs.
2. Following the curve of each fabric piece, stitch along one edge of each fabric pair to secure (using a ¼-inch seam allowance) and press the seam towards the darker piece. Pin another lighter piece to the other edge of the darker piece and sew along the pinned edge. Repeat process until you have two halves of the ball, each with two dark and two light pieces.
3. Pin the two halves with the right sides facing in – making certain to line up the top and bottom.
4. Leave about 5" of the bottom unpinned to allow room to stuff the ball.
5. Sew around the pinned edges, remembering to leave the opening for stuffing.
6. Turn the pillow right side out and stuff with fill until it forms a firm sphere.
7. Close the pillow using a simple blind stitch and sew on fabric-covered buttons to the ends of each sphere.

NOTE-WORTHY

At the flea market, give old, tattered books and journals a second look: Bring them home and dress them up with dyed cotton twill tape for newfound appeal..

YOU WILL NEED:
> **Old books with worn, damaged covers**
> **Lengths of several colors of dyed cotton twill tape (measure lengths to fit each book to be covered).**
> **Glue gun**
> **Hot glue sticks**
> **Scissors**

1. Chose the number of twill tape strips according to the size of each book.
2. Add 2 inches to all measurements and cut.
3. Lay the strips on a flat surface and weave, using the above photo as a guide.
4. Wrap the outside cover and glue the tape ends to the inside.
5. Finish the inside covers with fabric, card stock, or felt.

LIGHTEN UP

Channel your inner DIY skills and transform a not-so-attractive lamp from the flea market into one that steals the limelight.

YOU WILL NEED:
> **A wooden-based lamp (with shade), in safe working condition**
> **A drill and Forstner or wood spade bit (match the bit size to the diameter of the button)**
> **Old, fabric-covered buttons or a button-making kit (available at craft stores)**
> **Spray adhesive and a hot glue gun**
> **Dyed fabric and scissors**

1. Measure the diameter and depth of your buttons. Using the above photo as a placement guide, drill holes the required depth so that the button is flush with the surface. Remove all dust and wood shavings.
2. To make the shade, measure the height and perimeter of the shade, and allow for a ½ inch excess of fabric to fold onto inside rims.
3. Using those measurements, cut out the fabric and use a warm iron to remove any wrinkles.
4. Apply spray adhesive to the existing shade and carefully adhere the fabric, smoothing out wrinkles as you go.
5. Fold under the raw edges and use a hot glue gun to secure the top and bottom edges of the fabric to the inside of the shade.
6. To cover the buttons, follow the directions on the button-making kit, or drop fabric-covered buttons into dye mixtures.
7. When dry, use hot glue to adhere the buttons into the hollows of the lamp base.

MAKE IT We used these fiber reactive dyes from DharmaTrading.com for our projects: PR15, PR16, PR17, PR38A, PR49, PR61, PR86, PR 112.

Dyes are a vintage fashion lover's sensible best friend. Much-loved but tired items, like this thrift-shop woven tote (left), can be updated in companion shades of purple.

COLOR YOUR WORLD
Spring staples, like these light linen sneakers, go from shabby to chic with some new laces and a color dip. Heavier fabric and materials like canvas require longer soaking with more intense color to achieve adequate color saturation. Remove old laces before dyeing, and set sneakers (on newspaper or the grass) in the sun to dry. Spring is the perfect time to dye fabrics: Take a large, galvanized metal tub or container outdoors and hang items on a clothesline to drip-dry in the sun.

GREEK REVIVAL

Bargain-shop your way to rich, sophisticated style by blending pieces with classical lines—but without the high-cost lineage.

RAISE IT FROM THE RUINS

By scouring secondhand stores, flea markets, and architectural salvage shops you'll unearth a trove of treasures with ancient airs, such as this cement garden urn (opposite). Small vases, cups, and candlesticks carved from alabaster—a mineral that began to be popular for knickknacks in the 1940s—glow in the natural light. Completing the windowsill display is a plaster bust that was probably cast in the 1930s, when classical decorating was all the rage.

DUO IND

AD

SYNOPSIN METHODICA

MARTINI LI

QUO

PRIMUS CONCHYLIORUM CLASSES EXHIBET

EO IPSO ORDINE IN QUO DISPONUNTUR

A LISTERO.

ALTER EASDEM COMPLECTITUR JUXTA

METHODUM CELEBERRIMI

CAROLI A LINNE,

NEC NON

TABULAS LISTERIANAS ACCOMMODATUR.

OXONII,

TYPOGRAPHEO CLARENDONIANO,

M DCC LXX.

SET THE TABLE

Matthew snatches up lamps made from alabaster—working or not—and uses them to sculptural effect in tabletop groupings (above), where aged book plates, a milk glass bowl, and a small china compote with gilded edges complement the look of antiquity. Corral papers in timeworn white platters (opposite), and use a bust to keep them in place.

TIP Church fundraisers are particularly good sources for items with classical motifs, Matthew says. He bought this bust at a yard sale at a Greek Orthodox church.

WHISPER IT IN WHITE

Gathering together white and ivory items reinforces the classical look even if all the pieces, such as the metal candelabra, don't have Greco-Roman overtones. A fabric remnant is tacked against the wall in folds reminiscent of a toga, and it provides the backdrop for an antique etching. The model of the Acropolis was probably a school prop—and a steal for $10. Decorative spheres, a gilded cloche base, and a white-cloth-covered book add interesting texture to the one-color palette.

ELEMENTS OF THE LOOK

1. From a store that specializes in architectural salvage, these concrete spheres could dress a garden bed. But here they are pretty indoor features atop a gilded platform.

2. "One of my favorite things at a flea market is a table of 'smalls', which are odds and ends usually priced a dollar or less," Matthew says. That's where he picked up this bust, which he elevates to special prominence by placing it under a glass cloche.

3. Tag-sale books need not appeal just to your inner bookworm. They are decorative assets as well when you remove the tattered paper covers. Use them as pedestals for decorative objets, or fill a blank bookshelf with tomes of the same hue for a modern block of color.

4. This antique etching still has its original slender frame, but sometimes it's best to reframe secondhand art to give it a crisp new look.

5. Rustic and battered, this wooden model of a Greek ruin is charmingly imperfect. Matthew guesses it was a school project—for history or shop class—but it might have been a store display piece instead. Half the fun of decorating with flea market finds is inventing the back-story.

6. Less expensive than marble (in fact, it's often called "poor man's marble"), alabaster has similar veining and is luminous in the light. For that reason, it is often used to make lamp bases, which become inexpensive sculpture when you find them without the rest of the lamp. Urn-shape vases are another common shape.

TIP Alabaster is a soft, porous stone, so do not clean it with water. Instead, wipe it gently with a supple, dry cloth, and use a non-abrasive cleaning powder, such as Borax®, for stubborn stains.

SCULPT A STILL LIFE

Mantels, picture ledges, windowsills, tabletops, and even empty chairs become artistic backdrops for arrangements of like objects (opposite). Architectural elements, such as a gilded wreath from a fireplace surround and a portion of a radiator cover, underscore the framed pen-and-ink sketch of a cathedral. White-painted woodwork (this page) sets off the subtle colorations of alabaster and porcelain pieces, including an urn, a filagree bowl, and a ceiling medallion.

1 **2**

3

"There is value in the ruins. You can decorate on the cheap with pieces that are chipped, broken, or discolored, which only enhances their patina."
— *Matthew*

RUSH FOR GOLD

Gold and ivory pair naturally together, and Matthew often mixes gold-rimmed china or metallic picture frames into his classical groupings. A perfect complement is Syroco carvings—an up-and-coming collectible. Taking its name from the Syracuse Ornamental Company, which originally produced the decorative wood—and later resin—motifs, Syroco has come to describe any number of elaborate gold- or bronze-painted architectural embellishments. **1.** Bearing the true mark, this Syroco wall vase shows the detail of the real thing. **2.** Flea markets are rife with decorations wearing gold finishes, which makes them inexpensive to collect. **3.** Wearing a shiny new coat of gold armor, this medallion shines.

HOW TO GILD THE LILY

Found objects and collectibles—from art frames to bits of molding—can benefit from a brush with gold paint. You can spiff up the tarnished finish on a piece of Syroco, or cast an unfinished item, such as this salvaged architectural carving, in a new light. Check art stores for oil-based metallic paints in a variety of hues, from pale Champagne to hearty bronze. Prep the piece to be painted by cleaning all the nooks and crannies with tack cloth to remove any dust that would mar the finished look. Then lightly brush on the paint using a good-quality artist's brush, applying several thin layers rather than one thick one. "I've gilded chandeliers, embossed chair backs, moldings, and furniture edges," Matthew says. "Anything with a raised design really comes to life with gold enhancement."

1

2

3

HAPPY TOGETHER

Starting a collection of classical pieces is easier than you think. First, they should have a look of age, so the chips and cracks that make them inexpensive are desirable. Second, many themes and motifs work together, from urns to busts to depictions of ancient artifacts. "I like to mix styles," Matthew says. "Once you begin to assemble these mismatched items, they take on a look that support each other." **1.** Cluster items together—even if you have just a few—to give your collection more impact. And give them prominence with the display, either on an elevated stand, in a case, or on an important spot, such as the mantel.
2. A transferware plate with ancient scenes fits the look. **3.** Matthew bought a box of letters and cards at a flea market and loves the visual appeal of the old-fashioned script.
OPPOSITE: Odd elements become harmonious with a gentle theme: A wall rack conveys the arches of classical buildings; a metal finial shows off its urn shape; and a Wedgwood pitcher with a scroll pattern has the look of a curated museum piece thanks to the cover of glass.

THE EASTER HUNT

Usher in spring's most anticipated holiday with a celebration inspired by your prettiest flea market finds and the season's first blooms.

SPRING FORWARD

Set your Easter table with an assortment of mismatched dishes from the flea market – collected in a single color palette – and an assortment of early spring flowers. Apple blossom stems bloom from vintage wine decanters and spring-blooming hyacinths nestle in gold-rimmed glasses for instant spring color.

1 **2** **3**

FLOWERS AND TREATS APLENTY

An Easter celebration is incomplete without a few sweet treats and floral blooms. **THIS PAGE: 1.** Put a collection of vintage cookie cutters to use and make Easter cookies for guests to nibble on. **2.** Every flea market hosts a bevy of old baskets to choose from and can usually be found for under a dollar. To recycle as Easter baskets, simply vacuum away dust and line with shredded tissue paper. Embellish with millinery flowers from vintage hats, corsages, or nosegays. Simply remove the blooms from their stems before applying with hot glue. **3.** Old sap buckets can be revived with a color wash using flat-finish acrylic or poster paint. Use equal parts of paint and water and apply a thin coat to the container, then wipe off the excess with a clean cotton rag. Allow to dry, and recoat until you achieve the desired color. Fill with apple blossom stems and enjoy the sweet scent of spring. **OPPOSITE:** Egg-shaped lollipops are given vintage appeal by wrapping their sticks with colored seam binding and trimming with velvet millinery leaves.

FIND IT Damaged vintage hats, often overlooked by collectors, are a great way to glean millinery flowers without spending a lot of money.

"I draw inspiration from flea market finds for many of the paper crafts I make — like these party picks."
— *Matthew Mead*

GRAND STAND
A vintage pink Fenton cake stand (OPPOSITE) hosts warm brownies drizzled in buttercream icing and sprinkled in nonpareils. Paper flower picks—inspired by the pattern on the dinner plate pictured on page 144—can be recreated using the directions and downloadable pattern found on our website: HolidayWithMatthewMead.com.

MAKE IT Create this flower garland by hot-gluing millinery blossoms to a length of seam binding and drape along chairs or doorways.

TAKE IT OUTSIDE

Invite your guests out to the patio or terrace for a casual Easter lunch. OPPOSITE: A simple flea market camp table with folding legs is pressed into service, and its accompanying tag sale chairs – revived with a fresh coat of pink paint – are dressed for the occasion with floral garlands made using vintage faux flowers.

EASTER BASKETS
Proving one person's trash is another one's treasure, Matthew created delightful Easter basket party favors (THIS PAGE) by photographing a beautiful vintage tin trash can (OPPOSITE), and then printing the image onto heavy cardstock. To create your own, find the directions and downloadable pattern at HolidayWithMatthewMead.com.

1 2

3

PRETTY IN PINK

Dressing the table offers a plethora of
opportunity for using vintage collectibles
in a thoughtful and creative way.

THIS PAGE: 1. Early plastic party favor
bowls are filled with apple blossoms floating
in water. 2. Non-traditional place markers
can be fashioned using vintage spoons
sprayed with pink paint. Use scrapbooking
stickers or a metallic-ink pen to inscribe
guests' names onto the flatware and
place at each table setting. Packets of
old correspondence can be found at flea
markets and photocopied for use as place
mats or runners, offering quiet relief for the
pink dishes. 3. Tiny porcelain basket-weave
pots are planted with moss and tender
clover seedlings and serve as an enduring
take-away gift for each guest.

OPPOSITE: A delicate pink Bristol glass
vase is ringed in a circle of vintage silk
millinery flowers and filled with velvet
button flowers salvaged from a thrift-
shop boutonnière. To find similar millinery
supplies, shop vintage clothing stores,
flea markets, estate sales, online vintage
clothing shops, Etsy.com, or eBay.

FIND IT Merchants who deal in vintage holiday collectibles display relevant items months in advance, so start your search early!

SPRING BLOSSOMS

When using woody-stemmed florals, use a hammer to smash the stem at the cut end and insert into fresh water for arrangements that last up to 3-4 days. THIS PAGE: Fill a glass vase or vessel with floral branches, wrap with florist wire, and hang from a wooden door. OPPOSITE: Use collectibles like this vintage glass bunny as part of a whimsical centerpiece.

resources

COVER

Wall paint: "Refresh" by Sherwin-Williams (Sherwin-Williams.com)

Desk paint: "Bamboo" by PPG Pittsburgh Paints (PPGPittsburghPaints.com)

Fern stencil: TheStencilStudio.com

Rug: "Dandelion" by Company C (CompanyC.com)

WORLD HUES

1. "Australian Green" by Pratt & Lambert Paints (PrattandLambert.com). Take this custom formulation to your local paint store: B 1¾; D 1½; H 18; MY 6.

2. "Melville" by California Paints (CaliforniaPaints.com)

3. "Silver Dollar" by Benjamin Moore (BenjaminMoore.com)

4. "Glorious Sky" by Pratt & Lambert Paints

5. "Split Pea" by Pratt & Lambert Paints

6. "Light Sage" by PPG Pittsburgh Paints

7. "Equator Blue" by Pratt & Lambert Paints. Take this custom formulation to your local paint store: A8; J10; S 20½.

8. "Port Hope" by California Paints

9. "Ocean Blue" by Pratt & Lambert Paints. Take this custom formulation to your local paint store: A6; D1; J6; S ¾.

LILAC TIME

Wall paint: "Winter Dusk" by PPG Pittsburgh Paints

Printer fabric: Jo-Ann Fabric and Craft Stores (JoAnn.com)

GOT MILK

Wall paint: "Golden moon" by Valspar Paint (Lowes.com)

COOL DOODLE

Wall paint: "Corduroy" by Valspar Paint

Chalkboard paint: Lowes (Lowes.com)

Prints and photo enlargements: FedEx Office (FedEx.com/office)

BABY STEPS

Cupboard paint: "Bamboo" by PPG Pittsburgh Paints

Crib and changing table: "Refresh" by Sherwin-Williams

Frames: Rowland Studio (RowlandStudio.com)

Aqua-and-coral sparrows fabric: Warm Biscuit Bedding Co. (WarmBiscuit.com)

Rug: Dash & Albert Rug Co. (DashAndAlbert.com)

Tiered stand: Matthew Mead Collection (MatthewMeadCollection.com)

MID-CENTURY MATTHEW

Volkswagen print enlargement: FedEx Office

Upholstery: Pat Turgeon; P A Turgeon Upholstery, Boscawen, New Hampshire

Wall paint: "Bamboo" by PPG Pittsburgh Paints

FROND MOMENTS

Desk paint: "Bamboo" by PPG Pittsburgh Paints

Fern stencil: TheStencilStudio.com

Glass plates: A.C. Moore Arts & Crafts (ACMoore.com)

INDUSTRIAL REVOLUTION

Pages 82–83 chalkboard paint: Lowes (Lowes.com)

Pages 84–85 wall paint: "Yellow Strength" by Pratt & Lambert Paints

Page 86 wall paint: "Ethereal" by Pratt & Lambert Paints. Decal Letters: Ace Hardware (AceHardware.com)

Page 87 wall color: "Citronette" by Pratt & Lambert Paints. Striped rug: Dash & Albert Rug Co. (DashAndAlbert.com)

Page 88–89 wall color: "Red Carriage" by Pratt & Lambert Paints. Rug: "Nanping" by Company C (CompanyC.com)

FIT TO BE DYED

Dyes and dyeing supplies: Dharma Trading Co. (DharmaTrading.com)

Mat board: Michaels (Michaels.com)

Button kits: Jo-Ann Fabric and Craft Stores (JoAnn.com)

GREEK REVIVAL
Gilding paints: Michaels
(Michaels.com)

THE EASTER HUNT
Millinery flowers: Tinsel Trading
Co. (TinselTrading.com)

BLOGROLL
Holly Becker
Decor8Blog (Decor8Blog.com)

Jessica Bennett
Alice Lane (AliceLaneHome.com)

Kim Demmon
Today's Creative Blog
(TodaysCreativeBlog.net)

Sarah Egge
Adventures of the Cheapskate
Decorator (CheapDecorating.
blogspot.com)

Tricia Foley
(TriciaFoley.com)

Annette Joseph
(AJPhotostylist.net)

Amy Locurto
(LivingLocurto.com,
PrintablesByAmy.com, and
IHeartFaces.com)

Linda MacDonald
Restyled Home
(RestyledHome.ca)

Matthew Mead
(HolidayWithMatthewMead.com
and MatthewMeadCollection.
com)

Stephanie Nielson
The NieNie Dialogues
(NieNieDialogues.com)

Layla Palmer
The Lettered Cottage
(TheLetteredCottage.net)

Marian Parsons
Miss Mustard Seed
(MissMustardSeed.com)

Kate Riley
Centsational Girl (CentsationalGirl.
com)

Stefanie Schiada
Brooklyn Limestone (www.
BrooklynLimestone.com)

Jocie Sinauer
Red Chair Antiques (RedChair-
Antiques.com)

MATTHEW'S TOP 12 FLEA MARKETS

1. 127 CORRIDOR SALE
(127Sale.com). The world's
longest yard sale occurs between
Hudson, Michigan, and Gadsden,
Alabama. August 2–5.

2. Alameda Point Antiques
& Collectibles Faire
(AlamedaPointAntiquesFaire.
com) in Alameda, California. An
800-vendor show in northern
California, it's held the first Sunday
of every month, rain or shine.

3. Brimfield Antique Show and
Flea Market (BrimfieldShow.com)
in Brimfield, Massachusetts. In
2012, this premiere show will
occur May 8–13, July 10–15, and
September 4–9.

4. The Brooklyn Flea
(BrooklynFlea.com) in Brooklyn,
New York. Head to Fort Greene on
Saturdays from April to November,
or visit its indoor location at
Skylight One Hudson Place on
Sundays.

5. First Monday Trade Days
(FirstMondayCanton.com) in
Canton, Texas. Open the Thursday
through Sunday prior to the first
Monday of each month.

6. Kane County Flea Market
(KaneCountyFleaMarket.com) in
suburban Chicago. Head to this
large indoor/outdoor market the
first weekend of the month, March
through December.

7. The New General Store
(TheNewGeneralStore.com) in
Yaphank, New York. Dear friend
Tricia Foley curates these pop-up
sales on her Long Island property
for entire weekends in May and
November. Check the web site for
2012 dates.

8. Rose Bowl Flea Market
(rgcshows.com) in Pasadena,
California. Visit the famed Rose
Bowl stadium on the second
Sunday of every month.

9. Sage Farm Antiques
(SageFarmAntiques.com) in North
Hampton, New Hampshire. You
may run into Matthew at one of
these monthly sales, which have
different themes and occur the
first weekend.

10. Shipshewana Auction & Flea
Market (TradingPlaceAmerica.
com) in Shipshewana, Indiana.
Check out this huge outdoor
flea market on Tuesdays and
Wednesdays from May through
October.

11. Springfield Antique
Show & Flea Market
(SpringfieldAntiqueShow.com) in
Springfield, Ohio. Extravaganza
weekends in May and September.

12. Vintage Country Marketplace
(BarnHouseBH.com) in Battle
Ground, Washington. This small
but mighty occasional sale is put
on by the talented Barn House
Boys on July 28.

THRILL OF THE HUNT

"Early American glass domes aren't easy to find, so adding a new piece to my collection makes my heart skip a beat."
— *Matthew Mead*